# AVOIDING WEDDING AFTERSHOCK

OR

*I Like You Even Better Now That I Know You*

by Charlie Michaels
with Mike Brown

Family Matters Publications
North Hollywood, CA

*Printed in the United States of America*
Library of Congress Catalog Card Number: 90-081456
ISBN 0-9626525-0-4

# <u>We Can't Thank You Enough . . .</u>

With special thanks to those who have contributed both directly and indirectly to the evolution of this book:

Ken Burley who suggested that writing down our assumptions about marriage would be a useful exercise. It was the best wedding present you could have given us (although the tea set is nice, too!).

The Rev. Dr. Louis Gishler for marrying us and imploring that we choose to stay married to each other every day for the rest of our lives. See? Despite stars in our eyes, we were listening!

Mom and Dad, for being great parents and setting a colorful example of married life.

Our Grandparents who demonstrated that most of the time a loving marriage isn't a 50-50 proposition.

Kathy Westman Figler who started it all.

Bobbi Buford for her editorial comments.

John Buford, Nancy Buford, Lyn Corbett Fitzgerald, Sarah Flores, Elizabeth Gilham, Jan Helgeson, Stephanie Klebenow, Marnell Lloyd, Darla Lord, Carol Oldham, Wilda Quimby, Judith Roelse, Eva Smith, Floren Strope, Conness Thompson and Barb Zahn for their insights and words of encouragement.

Steve Whyle-Spitz, Andrew Kwee, Tony & Marilee Hyman for their technical support.

With love and heartfelt appreciation -

Charlie and Mike

# TABLE OF CONTENTS

We Can't Thank You Enough .................. 6

By Way of Introduction ....................... 7

Of Chocolate Covered Caramels ............... 13

Was It Just My Imagination? .................. 17

In Order to Form a More Perfect Union ......... 23

Get Your Pacts Straight ...................... 26

To Thine Own Self Be True ................... 31

On Your Mark, Get Set ...................... 36

A Penny for Your Thoughts .................. 42

The Heart of the Matter ..................... 81

I Never Said That! And If I Did ............... 90

You Just Can't Win ......................... 97

I Think I Need Glasses ...................... 104

When Does Your Warranty Expire? ............. 111

Say What You Mean, Mean What You Say ........ 116

Go Ahead. Make My Day! .................... 128

We're #1! ................................. 134

Thanks A Lot .............................. 143

If You Really Loved Me, You'd Eat Chinese ....... 150

A Final Word .............................. 156

Write Us .................................. 159

## DEDICATION

To Hueston Woods, mustard, grandfather clocks, oriental rugs, cinnamon-raisin English muffins, surface tension and all the other things that made us know we were exactly right for each other.

# By Way of Introduction . . .

Hi, my name is Carol, but I prefer to go by my nickname, Charlie. Following a meeting in 1980, a business associate took me aside and said he could tell by looking at me that a special fellow had entered my life whom he thought I would marry. He then gave me thirty seconds of advice that dramatically improved my chance for success in marriage.

He suggested we write down the assumptions we had about marriage.

Intrigued, I suggested to my fiance, Mike, that we give it a try. I wanted to give our marriage every chance of getting off on the right foot, but I didn't really think Mike would be interested. He was. In fact, he thought it sounded like a very good idea.

We decided the idea merited a weekend. In preparation, we individually wrote out our assumptions on every topic that came to mind.

Suddenly, I wasn't so sure I should have brought it up. Something inside me expected him to finally know all about me and dump me!  Talk about insecure - I still have the card I bought to send him if we broke up.

Saturday we began comparing our ideas.

It was an incredible two days. Fun. Heartwarming. Endearing. Hilarious. Occasionally infuriating - with a few moments of sheer panic. The things we learned about each other! No, we didn't agree on everything. But in our disagreement it was thrilling to experience each other's commitment to our relationship.

We laughed, we cried, we shared hopes, dreams, fears and secrets we hadn't trusted to anyone. Under all the passion and love that had been between us, we discovered that we really, *really, REALLY* liked each other.

Ultimately, we devised a list of mutual agreements. The result of negotiation and compromise, we called this our Marriage Pact and pledged to honor it.

It was the best investment either of us ever made. We eliminated many nagging doubts, honestly addressed problems we would face, nipped disagreements in the bud and set the stage to become best friends.

This book is an outgrowth of that weekend. We have been compelled to write it by family and friends who have marvelled that our marriage has flourished under far from ideal circumstances. We credit our success to commitments we made that weekend and have lived by during our marriage.

It's that simple. It can be that simple for you.

This is a practical hands-on guide: no theories, hypotheses, anthropological studies or educational treatises. No bull. Just a simple system that worked for us.

This book reveals, step by step, how we laid the groundwork for a marriage that has far exceeded our most optimistic expectations. We believe our simple process can work for you.

Your investment? The cost of this book and a few days of hard work. A small price when you consider the potential payoff: getting what you want from your marriage.

Our best wishes for your success,

Charlie Michaels
aka Mrs. Mike Brown

Mike Brown

Note: To eliminate the confusion of saying he/she, him/her, etc., I've alternated using he/him for one example and she/her for the next. No special meaning is intended. Please think of references to *you* as yourself and any reference to *he, she, him* or *her* as your partner.

**Differing expectations can cause problems to grow.**

# Of Chocolate Covered Caramels . . .

Wedding aftershock is the term we coined to describe the disorientation that occurs when the reality of married life is at odds with our expectations. Although none of the resulting confrontations may be earth shattering alone, collectively they can result in misunderstandings, hurt feelings and occasional chaos.

> *He expects her to do the shopping; she thinks they'll do it together.*
> *Thanksgiving's approaching and you've invited your family to dinner. Your spouse promised your in-laws you'd join their family gathering.*
> *Your charge card is rejected because it's over the credit limit. You didn't know anything was purchased.*

It's little comfort to know that all couples encounter some amount of post wedding trauma. Even when misunderstandings are amusing, it's disquieting to know you're not in sync. Some couples suffer so extensively their marriages fail before they have a chance to begin.

Most wedding aftershock can be eliminated by having a clear understanding of each other's expectations of marriage and by planning for the day-to-day aspects of married life.

Unfortunately, most couples spend more time selecting their china than planning their marriage. Perhaps that's not so surprising. After all, everyone knows they're expected to select a china pattern. It's an enjoyable task and relatively simple to do.

Who knows how to plan one's marriage? Where do you begin?

Some couples begin with prenuptial counseling. This is a good start, but doesn't go far enough. Prenuptial counseling focuses on the big picture: life goals, moral issues, should you marry. You are still left to ferret out the day-to-day issues yourselves.

Some couples are unable, unwilling or blind to the need to resolve the minor differences that create dozens of nagging little conflicts every day. Over time, these little irritations can make your marriage very uncomfortable - possibly even unbearable.

You may be familiar with the homily by Ben Franklin that goes something like this:

*A little neglect may breed great mischief . . . for want of a nail, the shoe was lost; for want of a shoe, the horse was lost; and for want of a horse, the rider was lost. For want of a rider, the battle was lost; and all for the want of a three penny nail.*

It's no joke. Little things really do mean a lot. When a major problem arises, the need to pull together is obvious. But as the saying goes, it was *the straw that broke the camel's back.* If you don't tend to the little things in your marriage, they may ultimately be your undoing.

Much of your happiness with married life will be determined by your expectations of marriage. This means that knowledge is happiness in marriage.

Think of your partner as a box of chocolates. If you think you have chocolate covered cherries, you'll feel disappointed if you come across a chocolate covered caramel.

When you know you have an assortment, you go into it realizing you'll like some selections better than others. That doesn't discourage you from indulging and loving it. You anticipate the variety and are more receptive to that occasional caramel.

The balance of this book is dedicated to helping you learn what comprises the unique assortment of your relationship . . . and preparing for those caramels. Years from now you may be surprised to find that some of those caramels have become very precious to you indeed!

# Was It Just My Imagination?

When you marry, the rules change. Your expectations of a spouse are different from those you had for a date.

Whether you're aware of it or not, each of us has been formulating a concept of the ideal spouse since childhood. These images are a composite of attributes observed through personal contact, movies, books, newspapers, television and other media - blended with a good dash of imagination.

The big lie: Nothing will change when we marry.

Although you may never have given it conscious thought, you know how your ideal spouse would:

. talk to you when you're down
. handle your birthday
. relate to your parents
. treat your friends
. dress

Even if you can't describe these in detail without prompting, you intuitively know how he'd act in every circumstance. Walk into a restaurant and look at the patrons - you'll judge who's dressed properly, whose table manners are appropriate, who's acting the right way. Go anywhere and watch any couple; you know when a husband or wife does something right or wrong.

If you carry the concept of the ideal spouse one step
further, you'll see why so many of us end up marrying
an image. And why so many couples end up disillusioned
as time goes by. You may fall into the trap of trying to
change your partner to match your ideal. If you're not
aware of what's going on and actively working to avoid
it, you almost can't help yourself!

No spouse will hold up well over time if constantly
compared to your ideal image. Your spouse isn't privy to
your imagination, so she has no way of knowing what's
expected of her. What you're expecting keeps changing
as your ideal image evolves through time.

We suggest you replace your images with something that
will work better for you - a realistic profile of your
partner.

**I'm sorry. We're not open to the public.
You'll have to select from our ready-made stock.**

21

Examining your expectations of marriage will help you uncover the reality of where your future mate differs from your image. These deviations are the "caramels" in your relationship.

Fortunately, not all caramels are bad news. Many will just be a point of difference and some will be a delightful surprise. One of the best caramels I discovered in Mike is the way he puts me on a pedestal. I always expected to be treated as an equal, but I must say I'm rather fond of the view from up here!

# In Order to Form a More Perfect Union . . .

You not only change the rules for your partner, you also change the rules for yourself when you marry. You have preconceived notions of how you should perform your role of spouse.

Most people can accept that their partner will not match their ideal image perfectly. They expect some differences and make allowances for shortcomings. Many of these same people have much higher standards for themselves. What they would perceive as a caramel in their spouse they see as a major flaw in themselves. Some people go to a great deal of effort to correct these flaws - often to the detriment of their relationship.

Most of us have no idea what our spouse wants, so we make assumptions based on our own idea of what makes the ideal wife or husband. Because we love our spouse so much, we often fear that we don't measure up to what they deserve. Instead of just being ourselves, we beef up our performance to become an even more perfect person for them.

In all likelihood, our image of an ideal husband or wife will differ significantly from our spouse's. Sometimes, as we work to become what we think is expected of us, we sacrifice the very qualities that attracted our spouse in the first place. We've all seen a life-of-the-party marry only to become quiet and reserved.

At times our good intentions can actually back-fire. If you feel a wife should keep a spotless home, you may spend many hours cleaning. A clean house may not be a top priority with your spouse. Not realizing your intentions, he may resent the time you spend cleaning and think of it as an obsession. What began as an act of love may ultimately alienate him.

Although role playing is self defeating, it's difficult to avoid. We all want desperately to be worthy of our spouse's love.

If you think you may be immune to the tendency to role play because of your education, wealth, self-esteem, confidence or social position, think again. _People_ magazine published this quotation regarding the divorce of one of the most prominent couples of our era: "This is not about him having affairs. This is about two egos wearing away at each other. The more she worked at what she thought he'd like, the less he liked it."

Keep in mind that your vision of the ideal spouse is unique to you and may bear no resemblance to what your partner is expecting. This may make it easier for you to be yourself in your marriage.

# Get Your Pacts Straight . . .

The Marriage Pact is the name we've given the rules that form the foundation of a marriage. Every marriage is governed by the rules of its Marriage Pact. Each Marriage Pact is a unique reflection of its marriage partners.

Where do these rules come from? From the experience of the marriage partners, their observations of other marriages or their preconceived notions and best guesses of what makes a good marriage.

Study any married couple and you'll see their Marriage Pact in action:

> How do they spend money? How much do they save? Do they always buy the best? Do they cook at home or eat out?
> Who takes out the garbage? Does the laundry? Walks the dog? Sorts the mail? Pays the bills?
> How do they reach decisions? How are disagreements handled? Who defers to whom?

Most Marriage Pacts develop haphazardly - generally by the trial and error merging of unspoken expectations. Consequently few couples know the rules of their marriage. This is a shame.

Think about it. It's a "Catch 22": How can you live up to rules when you don't know what they are? Or when you find you don't share the same ones?

Is it any surprise there are so many unhappy marriages?

Sometimes, each partner thinks she has a clear vision of the Marriage Pact. It may turn out that your visions are distinctly different - even when you are *positive* they are the same.

We were a perfect example of two people who thought they knew what the other was thinking and were totally wrong. Our biggest misunderstanding had to do with children, a subject we had discussed and thought we agreed on: Mike thought we agreed not to have any children; I thought we agreed to have at least one.

This issue was not readily resolved. Fortunately, most topics are much less controversial. Say that as you discuss your morning routines, you discover that one of you bounds out of bed at the first sound of the alarm and the other pushes the snooze alarm half a dozen times. You need to get up at 6:30 am. When will you set the alarm?

There are no right or wrong answers and no correct solutions to differences uncovered. The idea is to create solutions you both can live with and answer those questions that "little voice inside your head" keeps asking. Once common expectations are reached, you make a pact and agree to live by it.

If you take an active role in creating your Marriage Pact with your partner, you can align your expectations into the reality of your marriage. This will make it much more likely that both of you will get what you want from your marriage.

It is easiest to create a Marriage Pact before you are married: before you create barriers between yourselves; before an argument reveals you've broken a rule you didn't know existed. If you're not yet married, you are in the ideal situation. Create your Marriage Pact before your wedding and get your marriage off to its best possible start.

If you are already married you have a greater challenge, but perhaps a greater motivation. You have probably already discovered where some of your expectations differ from your spouse's . . . The rest of your lives together will hopefully be a very long time. Formalizing your Marriage Pact can help you smooth over trouble spots you may already be experiencing and can help minimize differences that haven't yet become problems. It can make your marriage an even more enjoyable place to be.

Beginning with the next chapter, you will be guided through the development of a Marriage Pact tailored to your needs. One that encourages each of you to flourish individually while providing common ground to grow together as a couple. One that can evolve with you as your marriage matures and your needs change.

When you are done, you will know each other better than many people who have lived together for years. At best you will have gained an exciting new perspective of each other and the way for true intimacy will now be open to you. At worst, you may discover irreconcilable differences that make it highly unlikely that your marriage can succeed. Even this has its bright side as it could save both of you years of doing time in an unhealthy marriage.

We wish all of you well in your marriages and hope this book will help you off to a good start. It would be great if we could guarantee your results, but we can't. The book can only be a start, because responsibility for implementing the ideas lies with you. You will have to rely on your experiences, your integrity and your desire for a successful marriage. Only you and your partner can guarantee your results.

Let the adventure begin! Good luck!

# To Thine Own Self Be True

The first step in developing your Marriage Pact is identifying what you want. Your first task is to make a list of your assumptions about marriage. The next chapter will guide you.

DO THIS ALONE.

Don't consult each other or hint what your responses are. Don't compare notes. It probably will work best if you are physically separated while you work.

At this point, don't worry about what your spouse wants. Trust that he'll tell you. Your job is to tell your partner what you want.

**Second-guessing your spouse's preferences
can make your relationship second-rate.**

We can't over-emphasize how important it is for you to explore your feelings. Don't try to second-guess what your fiance wants you to say. She wants you to be yourself. What is important to you? How do you feel? What are you looking for? What are your needs? Your wants? What will make you happy?

This is not an exercise about changing yourself. You're not looking to create a "Stepford Marriage" where partners have subordinated all personal interests for the good of the marriage or the benefit of their partners. You're not striving for subservience or submissiveness.

What you are striving for is a clear statement of who each of you are, so your marriage can reflect your personalities and allow you to thrive both individually and as a couple. Don't undermine your efforts by trying to be anyone but yourself.

Some of you may fear, as I did, that if anyone really knew you, they wouldn't want to marry you. I don't know if that's true or not. But even if it were true, eventually your spouse is going to know you. Then what?

I was terrified of letting *anyone* know my answers to all these questions. I felt incredibly vulnerable and was afraid that Mike would find me inadequate.

I finally decided to tell Mike all there was to know about me because I couldn't imagine what kind of life we'd have if I felt that I was hiding parts of me. I knew I'd be overwhelmed with uncertainty about the stability of our relationship because the *real* me wouldn't feel loved. I also knew I'd feel guilty at my deception.

A major advantage of creating our Marriage Pact was knowing that I am accepted and wanted just the way I am. It has freed me to love and be loved more completely. This knowledge of acceptance has been key to achieving intimacy in our marriage. It seems that this would be true for you as well.

If you are both straight forward and honest in preparing your assumptions, you will have given each other a tremendous gift - the key to making each other happy.

Don't blow it. Be honest.

# On Your Mark, Get Set . . .

Before you begin working on your Marriage Pact, we recommend that you read this book cover to cover for a complete understanding of the process. This will take most people less than three hours. When you're done, return to this chapter and do the exercises.

You'll start as we did by identifying assumptions you hold about being married, married life, your life goals and your role as a marriage partner. Then you'll compare your assumptions and negotiate your differences until you have created a list of assumptions you agree on. Your finished list is your Marriage Pact.

We told you our secret was simple!

To get started, you'll need paper and pen to write down your thoughts on the topics listed in the next chapter. We found it most convenient to use a notebook for easy reference and to keep everything together. When we developed our Marriage Pact, I used about thirty pages for my notes while Mike used about eight.

Questions on each topic are listed to help you identify your assumptions in each area. Related items are grouped together and have been listed alphabetically. It's not possible to list them in order of importance since that will vary from couple to couple.

How you handle your individual work is a matter of personal preference. Mike sat down and wrote out his assumptions in one fell swoop. I chose to spend several hours on several different days on mine.

Your answers will allow your partner to learn more about you and what you expect from her and your life together. Misunderstandings in the listed areas are often the source of problems for couples; this is a terrific opportunity to identify areas that are apt to be hot spots in your marriage.

It is virtually impossible for two people to agree on everything. Don't worry about it! What is important is that you know in advance where you don't agree and how you will cope with your differences.

Keep in mind that your objective is to outline your understanding of what your married life will be like. You want your comments to lead to complete discussions of each topic. It's to your advantage to be as specific as possible.

Write your assumptions for each topic using the items listed after the topic as a starting point. As other thoughts come to mind, jot them down as well. If you assume that things will be one way but would prefer them to be another way, state both your assumption and your preference.

It will be helpful if statements are self-contained so you do not need to refer to the book. For example, for the question: Will you/spouse smoke? You might say, "I assume that I will not smoke but you will smoke: I would prefer that neither of us smoked."

If you just say "No/no" or "No/yes but prefer no/no," you will have answered the question, but you'll have no idea what your answer means by itself. Being complete in your individual work will make it easier to compile your Marriage Pact.

For a question such as, "Will you/spouse work?" one possible answer would be, "I assume that both of us will work full time."

While this is an adequate response, this is a great time to ensure that your spouse is aware of your underlying feelings. You might want to elaborate: "I assume that you will remain in your job at ABC Company until someone offers you a better job. I assume you know that I hate my job. I will work full time but plan to send resumes to other companies when we get back from our honeymoon. Don't worry, I won't quit my job until I have something else lined up that pays at least as well."

This is your opportunity to have an audience. Take advantage of it - be heard!

You're now ready to write your assumptions on the topics in the following chapter. Don't pass anything over. An item that seems unimportant to you may be very important to your partner. Avoid problems: assume that each item is important to your partner, address it with the respect you would like to be accorded.

Even if you feel you've previously reached agreement on a subject, write down your understanding of it.

This is *not* a test. There are no right or wrong answers. Take your time. Be honest. Have fun.

One last comment. If you think it's going to be time consuming and sometimes difficult to answer all these questions, you're right. It will be. To put it in perspective, look at it this way: In the next seven days, most of you will spend forty hours earning a paycheck. Isn't your marriage worth more than a week's pay?

# A Penny for Your Thoughts

## About Me

Height, Weight, Hair color, Eye color, Birth date, Astrological sign, Color season
Social security #, Driver's License #
Clothing (brand, color, size)
   His:   hat, jacket, shirt, pants, belt, gloves, socks, shoes, suit/sport coat, top coat, undergarments

   Hers:  hat, jacket, blouse, pants, belt, gloves, hose, socks, shoes, skirt, dress, suit, coat, lingerie, pierced ears

## Affection

What non-sexual ways do you like to be touched? How many hugs do you like/need in a day?
Are there any ways that you do not like to be touched?

Do you like to hold hands, hug or kiss in public? When is it inappropriate to show affection?

Is it OK for your spouse to ask you to be hugged?
If your spouse wants to hold hands, be hugged, etc. how should he let you know?

Do you plan to hug, kiss, hold hands with, put your arm around anyone other than your spouse once you are married? Who will you do these things with?

If your affection to others causes your spouse to be jealous, how should he tell you? Will you stop doing it?

## Alcohol & Drugs

Do you/spouse drink alcoholic beverages? Use drugs? Have you in the past? What kind? How often? How much do you spend in a week?

Has your drinking/drug use ever been a problem? Caused you to miss work? Be arrested?

Have you ever been involved with Alcoholics Anonymous or other support group for users?

Do you mind if others drink or do drugs? Will your guests be allowed to drink or do drugs in your home? If you feel strongly against alcohol or doing drugs, do you ever find it acceptable? What types? When?

Are you currently taking any prescription drugs? What for? Are they optional?

What role do you want your spouse to play if she sees you becoming dependent on drugs or alcohol? What role do you want to play if you see your spouse getting into trouble?

Who will abstain and be the designated driver when you drink or do drugs away from home?

If you/spouse drink or do drugs, will you/spouse stop during pregnancy?

**Be sure you fully explore each other's assumptions.**

## Bad Habits

What are your odd or bad habits? What things about you have driven your parents, siblings and former roommates crazy?

Are you trying to break a bad habit at this time? Is there anything your partner could do to help you accomplish this goal?

## Birth Control

Does your religion place restrictions on use of birth control or abortion? What are they?

Will you use birth control? What form? What risks are associated with this form? Are there other forms you would consider using?

Would you consider sterilization of you/spouse after you have children?

What will you do if you/spouse becomes pregnant in spite of birth control?

What are your views on abortion? Would you ever consider an abortion for you/spouse? Under what circumstances? How late in pregnancy?

# Children

**BASICS:**
Do you like kids? Do you want to have any? How many?
When? Prefer son(s) or daughter(s)? Would you like to
follow practices designed to improve your chances of
having male/female children?
How do you feel about being a parent? What will you do
best as a parent? Least well?
What's your favorite age child? Least favorite age?

**CHORES:**
Who will teach your children their life skills? (How to
make bed, clean room, take out garbage, yard work, wash
car, do laundry, cook, dress, bathe, household repairs)
What chores will your children be expected to do? At
what age? Will you pay them? How much?
Will you expect your children to get jobs? At what age?
How may they use their earnings?

**CULTURALIZATION:**
Whose family customs will you follow daily? At
holidays? What are these customs? What nationality will
your children be? What languages will your children
speak?
What religion will your children follow? Will they attend
services? How often? Receive religious education? Be
baptized? Bar mitzvah? Confirmation?

**DAILY CARE:**
Will you/spouse work outside the home after the baby is
born? If so, how soon after baby's birth? Who will take
care of baby while you/spouse work? Who will take care
of children weekday evenings? Weekends?
Who will change diapers? Dress baby? Feed baby?
Will you/spouse breast feed baby? How long?

# Children, cont:

**DISCIPLINE:**
Who will discipline your children? How? Will you spank them? When? How much leeway should children have before they are disciplined verbally? Physically?
Will your parents or others be allowed to discipline your children? If so, who? How? Will boys and girls be disciplined the same? What bedtimes and curfews will you set in preschool? Grade School? Jr. High? High School?

**EDUCATION:**
Will your children go to day care? What age? Where?
Will they go to public or private schools?
Is there a particular school you want them to attend?
Do you want your children to go to college? Where?
When and how will you save to pay for private school or college expenses?

**ENTERTAINMENT:**
What kinds of things do you see yourself/spouse doing with your children? Will you play together? How?
Will your children go with you when you go out or will you hire a sitter? When? Who?
Will you take vacations with or without the children?
Will you restrict your children to age-appropriate activities or let them do grown-up things? (eg, take young children to see R-rated movies)
How much TV per day? Who will monitor acceptability of TV shows?
Will you read to your children? Who? How often? When?
What type of music will you expose your child to?

# Children, cont:

### EXPECTATIONS:
What do you expect of your children in general?
Any scholastic, athletic, social and career expectations?
Any sports they *must* play? Must not play? Are too dangerous? What if child doesn't want what you expect? Would you like your child to play a musical instrument? Which one?

### MEDICAL:
Is there a family history of twins, birth defects, retardation or problem pregnancies? Any reason you may not be able to have children?
Would you consider: Foster parenting? Artificial insemination? In vitro fertilization? A surrogate mother? Would you consider adoption? If so, any limits on child's race, health, sex, age, heritage?
Have you ever been pregnant or made someone pregnant? Ever miscarry? Had an abortion? Given a child up for adoption?

### NAMES:
Are there special names you want to give your children? What are they?
What surname will your children use?

### PROBLEMS:
Do you have any reason to suspect that you may not be a fit parent? That you might physically abuse your child? Do you have the patience to be a parent?
Will you disagree or argue in front of your kids?
What would you do if you discover your child is using drugs? Having sex? Missing school? Stealing? Fighting? Lying? Cheating? Would you consider getting professional help/family counseling?

# Children, cont:

## SOCIAL DEVELOPMENT:
At what age should children wear make-up? Begin dating? Get pierced ears? Wear adult clothing? Own car? Should children be taught about sex? Contraception? Disease prevention? At what age? By whom? How?
What will you do or not do to foster self-esteem?
How will your child address adults? Family? Friends? Relatives? At what age will you teach table manners? Etiquette? Social skills? Who will teach these?
When and how will you teach values? Work ethic? Money skills? Respect for others? Respect for property? Who will do this?

## STEPCHILDREN
How many are there? What ages? How well do you get along? How do you feel about them?
Where will they live? How often will you see them?
Who will discipline them? Pay child support, college expenses, costs of weddings, visits, joint vacations? Who will communicate with the children's other parent?
What relationship will children have with natural grandparents? Stepgrandparents?
What will they call their stepparent? Stepgrandparents? Would stepparent like to legally adopt them?

## YOUR CHILDHOOD:
Who raised you? Was your household male or female dominant? What was your home life like?
What responsibilities did you have at home? How did you feel about them? Do you want your children to have more, less, same amount of responsibility?
What school/community activities did you participate in?
What were important influences in your upbringing?
What did your parents do best as parents? Least well?
What specific things did your parents do in raising you that you want to do in raising your kids? Not want to do?

## Citizenship

What is your citizenship?

Do you donate time or money to community activities? Charitable groups? How much? To what?

Are you patriotic? What does this mean to you? What are your views on military service?

## Communications

Are you a talker or quiet type? If there is a pause in the conversation, are you likely to fill it? How do you feel about quiet people/talkers?

When do you like to talk? Are there times when you like to be left alone?

If your partner needs to talk and feels you aren't listening, what should she do to get your full attention? When and where should she approach you?

When you have something important to discuss, do you communicate best verbally or in writing? If one of you prefers verbal and the other written communication, how will you communicate?

Where do you like to have a good talk? Any places you don't want to talk seriously (eg, in bed)?

What do you like to talk about?
What will be difficult for you to discuss?
Are there any subjects you agree not to discuss? Which ones?

# Death

When you die, do you want to be buried? Cremated? Do you want to donate your organs? Which ones? Do you want a funeral service? Wake? Party? Do you want a big budget or economy send off? Are your wishes at odds with those of your family? If there's a disagreement, should spouse insist on your preferences or give in to family pressures? How strongly do you feel about this?

How long should your partner wait to date? Remarry?

Do you have a will? Where is it? What are the general terms of your will? Will you make a new will when married? What will the new terms be?

Do you have a life insurance policy? Who is the beneficiary? Will this change when married? Do you have burial insurance?

# Decision Making

How will you decide who gets her way on all the little things that come up? (eg, which restaurant you'll go to, who will be invited to your housewarming, how dressed up you'll get for the party at Smith's, where you'll buy your mother's birthday present, what style and color phone goes in the living room, which TV show to watch, which vanity you'll buy for the bathroom, which towels you use everyday . . .)

How will you resolve disagreement on major issues? (eg, will you buy a new car or fix your present car, will you take a European vacation or make a down payment on a house . . .)

## Ecology

How important is ecology to you?

Are you involved in any ecology efforts at this time? Which ones? Do you want to be more involved? How much time/money do you devote? Want to devote?

Will you recycle? What? Use disposable diapers? Styrofoam containers? Conserve water?

## Education

Do you have all the education you want to have?

If you or spouse plan to go to school, how will you finance it? What will your education cost? What's the payback?

If you go one at a time, who gets to go first? When does the other person get to go?

What degree or certificate are you aiming for? If your spouse works to put you through your degree does he have a right to feel he owns part of your degree?

Are you interested in taking adult education or other non-degree courses? What subjects?

## Emotions

What do you do when you are angry? How do you want your spouse to react to your anger?

How do you fight? What can your spouse do to avoid a fight?

Are you good at forgiving and forgetting? What can you do to become a more forgiving person?

What do you do when you are being selfish? Unreasonable? Hurt? Sad? Depressed? How would you like your spouse to treat you during these times?

What can your spouse do to show emotional support?

What do you do to relax or shake off the blahs?

What do you do when you're happy? What things make you happy? What do you do when you're frightened? What scares you?

## Employment

Do you/spouse work? For whom? What do you/spouse do? How will you get to work?

Are you in a union? What is the strike history? How do strikes affect you? When is your contract renegotiated? Strike likely? During a strike, what income do you have?

**Are there any family expectations?**

54

## Employment, cont:

What hours do you work? How much overtime? When is overtime most likely? Are you paid straight salary, commission, hourly or a combination? Explain.

Do you travel for your job? Where? How often? How long? Could spouse go along? What if spouse insists you find a job with little or no travel?

What are job benefits? Drawbacks? How happy are you with your current job? Would you like to change jobs? Is a promotion for you/spouse likely to require relocation? Are you willing to relocate for your promotion? Spouse's promotion? What happens if your spouse *must* relocate to find a job and you are *very* happy with your job?

What is your career objective? Any job dreams/fantasies? How will you feel if your spouse's career progresses faster than yours? Slower? How do you feel about your spouse's time commitment for career success? How does spouse feel about your time commitment for success?

Does either of your families have a business they hope you/spouse will become involved in? Does family business appeal to you? Do you feel you have a choice?

Is it OK for you/spouse to take a cut in pay to take a job that offers more personal satisfaction? Ever hope to start your own business? Doing what? Why don't you do it? If your spouse wanted to mortgage your home to start a business, would that be OK with you?

How important to you are company benefits like health/life insurance, dental plan, retirement plan?

Have you ever been fired or laid off? How would you cope with financial obligations? Emotional aftermath? How would you want spouse to react?

## Family & Relatives

What is your relationship with your family? Spouse's family? Have your families met? Do they get along? If they've not met yet, do you think they'll get along?

How often do you see or talk to your family now? Spouse's family? How often will you see them once you're married?

Will you visit parents and relatives separately or together?

What relationship do you want your spouse to develop with your family? What relationship do you hope to develop with spouse's family?

Does your family count on you for money? Health care assistance? Companionship? Grandchildren? How do you plan to meet these needs in your marriage?

Have you talked openly with your family about how your marriage will affect your relationship with them? Will you talk to them before your wedding? Alone or together?

How far away do you live from your/spouse's relatives? How do you feel about this? Would you ever turn down a job opportunity because it would cause you to move too far away from/too close to family or relatives?

What's the farthest you've ever been from home? Longest you've been away from your family? Longest you'd ever want to be away from your family?

Have you ever lived on your own? Been financially independent? When? How long?

## Finances

How important is money to you?

What sources of income do you/spouse have? How much will you/spouse earn this year? Will this change when you marry? Whose money is it?

Will you maintain separate and/or joint bank accounts? Charge cards? What expenses will be paid from each?

Do you have credit cards? Checking, savings, credit union account? What are the balances on your accounts?

IF YOU HAVE ASSETS YOU WANT PROTECTED, YOU NEED A LEGAL DOCUMENT. SEE AN ATTORNEY OR ACCOUNTANT *BEFORE* YOU MARRY.

Do you like to make safe investments or do you enjoy taking financial risks? Under what conditions would you risk everything you own?

Who will keep track of bills? Write checks? Who will do your taxes?

What debts and on-going financial commitments do you have? Child or parent support? Alimony? Student loans? Car or house payment? Medical bills?

Have you ever had bad credit? Been refused a loan or credit card? Ever been bankrupt?

What do you expect to earn five years from now? What income in today's dollars would make you happy? What is the most money you think you'll ever make in a year?

## Finances, cont:

How much spending money will each of you have
weekly? At what dollar value will you discuss
expenditures before making them? How will you decide
if you will buy something? If you can't agree, will you
buy anyway? What items over $500 do you aspire to
own?

What quality will you buy for self, spouse, home,
children? How much do you spend on a typical outfit
for casual? Business? Pair of shoes? Typical accessories?
How much do you spend on clothing monthly?

How will household expenses be budgeted? Will you
write out a budget? How much will you save monthly?
What will you save for?

How much do you spend each month on phone calls,
visits, entertaining? How much do you spend on
vacations, work-related expenses, eating out, lunches,
clothing, donations, groceries, hobbies, life/health
insurance? How do you use credit? For what? Will this
change once you're married?

If money gets tight, where will you cut corners? How far
back are you willing to roll if ill-fortune/financial
disaster hits?

## Fitness

Is fitness important to you? How do you rate your personal fitness? What would you like it to be? What are you doing to change it?

What exercise do you do regularly? Any sports? Can partner participate in your routine?

What can spouse do to support your fitness efforts? What should spouse do if he notices you getting out of shape?

Are you happy with your weight? If not, what can partner do to support your efforts to lose weight? Have you weighed ten pounds more than you do now? When?

How would you feel if you/spouse gained a great deal of weight after marriage?

If you plan to share a chore,
a written schedule will avoid confusion.

## Food

What are your favorite foods? What food allergies or strong dislikes do you have?

Do you like Italian dishes? Chinese? Japanese? Mexican? Indian? What other types do you enjoy/dislike?

How many meals and snacks do you eat each day? What do you typically eat for breakfast, lunch, dinner, snacks?

Who will do the cooking? When you cook, do you like anyone else in the kitchen? How good a cook are you?

Have you ever had anorexia nervosa or bulimia? Are you a binge eater? Have you ever been?

## Friends

Do you feel you can have separate friendships rather than couples only friendships? How about opposite sex friendships? Any jealousy?

Will you stop seeing any of your friends after you're married? Which ones? Why? Any of spouse's friends you expect spouse to stop seeing after marriage? Why? What will you do when you're with your friends?

What ongoing commitments do you have? Team sports? Clubs? Alumni group? Business organizations?

How many nights a week do you plan to spend alone with friends? With spouse and friends? How can your spouse become involved in your activities with your friends?

# Gifts

When do you expect to receive gifts?

What type of gifts do you want/not want to receive from spouse? Children? Do you like to give gifts you have made? Receive home made/ hand made gifts?

To whom and for what occasions do you give gifts? How much do you spend on gifts? Will this change once you get married?

When will you buy gifts for your children? How much will you spend per holiday as infants? In preschool? Grade school? High school? College? When they're adults? Will you buy them toys/clothing for no special occasion if child asks for them or because you feel like it? Who else may buy children gifts? Will you restrict quantity, content or value of these gifts?

What is your idea of a fabulous big gift your spouse could buy you someday? What little gifts might your spouse buy you just to let you know you're loved?

Do you expect to give/get an engagement ring? What do you expect it to be?

# Goals

Is there anything that you've always wanted to do? Any dreams or fantasies? A goal you want to achieve?

## Health

Do you feel you are in good health? What health problems do you have or have you had?

Have any blood relatives had heart disease, diabetes, alcoholism, stroke, sickle cell anemia, allergies, or any other health problem which might indicate that you're at risk?

What are you doing to minimize your health risks? What do you want your spouse to do to support your efforts?

What blood type are you? Do you have health insurance? With whom?

## Heritage & Culture

What is your cultural heritage? What role did this play in your upbringing? What role does it play in your life today?

What languages were spoken in your home? What languages do you speak? Understand? Do any of your relatives not speak English?

What prejudices do you have regarding race? Religion? Color? Creed? Education/intelligence? Physical attributes? Section of town? Parts of the country? Foreign countries? Foreign visitors?

## Hobbies

What are your/spouse's hobbies?

How much time and money do you spend on each hobby each month? How much time and money would you like to be able to spend?

Do you want your spouse to participate in your hobbies? How? Do you want to participate in spouse's hobbies?

## Holidays

Which holidays are important to you? Do you get time off at holidays? Which ones?

How do you currently spend these holidays? Where do you want to spend these holidays once you're married? Who do you want with you? When conflicts arise, how will you decide where you'll go or who will join you for holidays?

Would you consider celebrating a holiday early or late in order to be with the ones you love?

## Home

Where will you live initially? Where do you aspire to live? Do you want a second home? Where? When?

Will you rent or buy your home at this time? Do you hope to buy in the future? When? Would you like to buy an apartment? Condo? House? Town house? Mobile home? Are there any of these you would not consider living in? If you want to buy, what sacrifices are you willing to make?

What style of furniture/art work would be in your ideal home? What type of architecture would it be? What size home would you like to have?

Will anyone other than spouse live with you? Under what conditions would you allow others to live with you?

Are there places in the home or possessions you want to retain as *yours* when married?

## Home Maintenance

Will you do this yourself or pay someone to do it? Will your spouse help?

What skills do you have? Do you plan to learn any additional skills? Which ones?

**Don't worry if your friends aren't comfortable with your agreements. They don't have to live with them.**

# Household Chores

What level of cleanliness do you expect?

Who will do the cooking? Regular cleaning? Heavy cleaning (window washing, clean garage, spring cleaning)? Grocery shopping? Clothes shopping for you/spouse? Take out trash? Laundry? Ironing? Child care? Yard work? Household maintenance? Make bed? Change sheets? Pick up house? Change light bulbs? Bring in paper? Other chores?

What chores do you currently do for yourself or have others do for you that you expect your spouse to do when you marry?

# Illness & Injury

Should spouse comfort or ignore minor accidents and illnesses?

What should your spouse do in the event of a medical emergency? If doctors say there is no hope for your recovery and you will be a vegetable, do you want extraordinary measures taken to keep you alive?

If your illness were not covered by insurance, how much of your own money would you spend to try and save your life if you thought you could recover completely? If you thought you'd be mentally competent but physically paralyzed? If you thought you'd be a vegetable?

What would you expect to do in the above situations if your spouse were sick or injured?

# Leisure Pursuits

Are you athletic? What sports do you like to play/watch? How often?

How do you keep abreast of current events? What magazines, newspapers, types of books do you read?

What types of dancing do you enjoy? How often? Are you a skilled dancer?

What types of music do you enjoy? How often? Any types you can't stand? Do you like background music or do you only play music when you focus on it?

Do you like to play cards? How often? What games? Do you know how to play bridge? Poker? Board games? Do you like them? Do you belong to a card club? Want to?

Do you like to gamble? How do you feel about gambling? Do you play the lottery? Bet at the track? How much money do you spend weekly?

Do you prefer staying home or going out? How often do you like to go out? Do you like to get dressed up or prefer casual? What is *dressed up* and *casual* to you? Are there times, meals or events when it's important that you and your spouse be at home? Out on the town? When?

Do you like to go to parties? Give them? What types do you like to give or attend? How many people would be at your ideal party? How often do you entertain? Will this change when you marry?

How many hours do you watch TV a day? What types of shows do you like? Dislike? Favorite shows?

How often do you go to the movies? Would you like to go? Do you watch TV movies? How often? What types?

## Names

What name will you/spouse use after marriage?

Are there any nicknames you like being called? Dislike?

## Pet Peeves

What things drive you crazy in general? (Remember, this is not about making your partner over. It's OK to say that a messy house drives you crazy, but not OK to say that your partner's sloppiness drives you crazy. Once identified, each of you may see things you can do so that your actions don't aggravate the other's pet peeves.)

What things about your parents or relatives drive you crazy? Are you afraid you're going to do some of these things yourself? Which ones?

What do you want your spouse to do if you start picking up some of these irritating habits?

## Pets

How many and what kinds do you/spouse have? What if both of you have pets and they don't get along?

Do you want pets? What kind?

How much time does your pet take each day? Who will feed, exercise, clean-up after, groom pets?

What will you do when you're gone for a day? A week? Where will your pet stay during the day? At night?

How much money do you spend on food and vet bills for your pet each month? How much money would you be willing to spend to save your pet's life? Spouse's pet's life?

If your partner feels the pet is getting more of your attention than he is, does the pet go?


## Politics

Do you vote? Do you belong to a political party? Are you politically active? How?

How much time and money do you devote to politics? How much time and money would you like to devote?

Are you conservative? Liberal? What services do you feel government should provide? Not provide?

Do you object to your spouse belonging to a different political party? Voting for an opposing candidate?

# Privacy & Secrets

With whom will you share details of your personal life, disagreements, secrets, successes? Parents? Friends?

Will you keep secrets from each other? About what?

Does your job require discretion or secrecy? Why? Does this special knowledge you have put you or your family in danger?

# Religion

What role did religion play in your family? What religion?

Do you believe in a Supreme Being?

What role does religion play in your life now? What religion? How often do you attend services? How much time and money do you donate? Do you say grace at meals? Pray regularly? Is it important that your spouse join you in these activities? Do you want your spouse to convert to your religion? When? How important is this to you?

Do you want to be married in a religious service?

How do you see religion in your marriage? What expectations does your religion place on your marriage? Are these important to you?

How would you feel if your spouse decided to join a church or synagogue? Change religious affiliation? Drop her religious affiliation?

# Roles

Which of the following roles are you expecting to play in your marriage? When? Which are you expecting your spouse to play? When?

| | | |
|---|---|---|
| Arbitrator | Friend | Mechanic |
| Bookkeeper | Gardener | Nursemaid |
| Bottle Washer | Hair Stylist | Parent |
| Breadwinner | Handyman | Secretary |
| Comedian | Host/Hostess | Shopper |
| Companion | Housekeeper | Snow Shoveler |
| Cook | Laundress | Status Symbol |
| Errand Runner | Lover | Taxi Driver |

# Routines

**MORNING:**
What time do you need to get up? When do you set the alarm? What is your routine from the first time the alarm goes off until you are out the door? Note approximate times for each step.

**WORKDAY:**
Outline a typical day from the time you leave the house until you arrive home at the end of the day. If you are home during the day, describe how your time is spent.

**EVENING:**
What is your evening routine from the time you get home until you go to sleep? Note approximate times for each step. If you have once a week chores note when you generally handle them.
What side of the bed do you sleep on? What position do you sleep in? (On back, left or right side, stomach?)

**WEEKEND:**
What is your Saturday routine? Sunday routine? Outline typical weekend days.

## Sex

What are some things you find especially attractive about your spouse? Is there anything your partner can do to increase your attraction to him?

Will you talk about sex? Will this be easy for you? If your partner wants to tell you something about your sexual relationship, when, where and how is the best way to approach you?

What sexual experience have you had? Are you a virgin? Do you have any illnesses or take medications which may affect sexual performance?

Do you have any sexual fantasies? Do you hope to act them out? What role can your partner play? What happens if your partner doesn't want to act out your fantasies?

Will you/spouse be sexually exclusive to each other? What happens if someone has an affair? Will it end your marriage?

How often do you envision having sex after marriage? What will you do when you want sex but your partner's not in the mood? When partner wants sex but not you? Who will initiate sex?

Do you masturbate? Will you masturbate when married? Do you always have an orgasm? How do you feel when you don't climax? What can your partner do?

Ever had a venereal disease? Herpes? Warts? Ever been tested for AIDS? Exposed to AIDS? Would you like you and your partner to be tested for AIDS?

You may find you become a prisoner of your deceptions.

## Skeletons in Your Closet

Is there anything anyone has on you that they could use as blackmail? What?

Are there any irritating or embarrassing stories your spouse will hear from family, friends, co-workers? Anything you're ashamed of? Anything you wish were different about you?

Has anyone in your family been a victim of child abuse, or a child abuser? Abuse drugs or alcohol? Have a serious illness? Legal problems? Anyone in jail? Divorced? Anyone you'd just as soon your spouse not meet? Why?

What deceptions have you been carrying on with your partner? Are there things you've been doing for him that you don't usually do? (eg, Are you generally a slob but you've managed to keep your place neat as a pin when your partner's been around? Do you hate wearing make-up but have worn it every time you've been together?) Any fronts you're not sure you can keep up for the rest of your life?

Now is the time to talk about anything that you've been avoiding telling your partner. If these haven't come up already, talk about prior engagements, marriages, sexual relationships, inter-racial or inter-faith dating, brushes with the law, jail, school problems, drug, alcohol, gambling problems, children . . .

## Smoking

Do you/spouse smoke? Chew tobacco? Smoke cigar, pipe, marijuana? Have you ever?

If you are non-smokers, are you bothered by smoking? Will you ask guests not to smoke in your home? Do you prefer a smoke-free work environment?

If you smoke, will you stop smoking during your/spouse's pregnancy? Will you smoke after you have children?

## Talents

What are your personal strengths? What skills are you most proud of?

What skills would you like to develop further? How can your spouse support your efforts?

## Telephone

Do you like to talk on the phone? How much time do you spend on the phone each day? Are there any people you talk to regularly? Who? How often? For how long?

How many phone lines will you have? Will you have a separate children's line?

Who will answer the phone? What greeting will they use? Will you have an answering machine?

Who will you call long distance?

## These are a Few of My Favorite Things

Car                Color
Flower             Type of Jewelry
Meal & Snack       Memory
Musical Group      Night Out
Number             Song

What are some of your favorite things? Do you want your spouse to share these things with you? How?

Do you like to shop? For what?

## Things You Can Do
## To Show Me You're Sorry

Sometimes it's difficult to be the first to say you're sorry - or to accept your spouse's apology. You may find it helpful to identify things you can do for each other to help salve the wounds - like buying a pint of your favorite ice cream or picking up a paperback by a favorite author.

If you have difficulty finding the right words but don't want things to drag on as long as it might take to locate a pint of ice cream or an open bookstore, you may find it helpful to agree on a small gesture you can make to show each other you're ready to apologize. A simple but unusual action will work well - like wearing a safety pin on your collar or placing a dinner plate on the coffee table. The act itself is not important; the significance the two of you give it is important.

## Things We Like To Do Together

List dozens of things here. It probably won't seem possible, but the day will probably come when you'll be bored silly and unable to think of anything fun to do. Having this list can bring back great memories and set off delightful escapades!

## Unemployment

What are your thoughts on use/abuse of the welfare system? Food stamps?

Have you ever been unemployed? What were the circumstances? How did you feel? Are you likely to be unemployed in the future?

How would the bills get paid if you/spouse were unemployed?

## Updating Your Marriage Pact

How often will you review your entire Marriage Pact?

If your partner feels part of your Marriage Pact is not working, when, where and how is the best way to approach you to review this portion of your Marriage Pact? (The *I Think I Need Glasses . . .* chapter gives additional direction.)

## Vacations

How much paid vacation time do you get? How would you like to spend it? Where? Will you vacation separately, as a couple, with family or friends?

Will you save for big vacations or little weekend get-aways? Will you pay cash or charge your vacations?

How often will you take big budget vacations? What is your idea of a well-spent big budget vacation?

How do you like to travel? Car? Train? Bus? Boat? Plane?

## Vehicles

Do you drive? What? Ever have an accident?

How many do you have? Car? Truck? Van? RV? Boat? Motorcycle? Plane? How many do you want?

How often should you/spouse be able to get a different vehicle? Do you buy or lease? Pay cash or buy on credit? Buy new or used? How much do you spend for a vehicle?

How important are your vehicles to you? To your job?

## Wedding

What type of wedding do you want? Where? How many people would attend? What would you/spouse wear? How many bridesmaids and groomsmen would you have? What do your parents want for you? How important are their wishes to you?

Who will pay for wedding? What can you afford? Are you willing to go into debt for your wedding? If someone offered you cash to elope rather than have a formal wedding, would you take it?

Who do you want at your wedding? In your wedding? Whose feelings will be hurt if not included?

Will you/spouse wear wedding ring? Do you want to take a honeymoon? Where? How long? What can you afford?

Are you ready to get married now? If not, when?

# The Heart of the Matter

When both your lists of assumptions are complete, you are ready to draft your Marriage Pact.

Find a quiet, private place where you will have no interruptions - no family, no friends, no children, no phone, no pets. We rented a cabin for the weekend to be sure we'd be alone. Discussions generated may be lengthy. It may take you several days to cover all topics.

Sit down together. Review every item and every additional comment or assumption you noted.

Take turns being the first to share your comments. Start with a topic that seems non-controversial to both of you. One of you begins by reading his notes on that topic out loud to his partner exactly as written. Then the partner reads her notes on that topic.

If you are in agreement, confirm your position, eg: "We agree that we would like to have two children. If either of us is unable to have children we will pursue all other available options including adoption and artificial insemination but not a surrogate mother."

Enter this mutual assumption, this agreement, on a new list. This list will recap your agreements about your marriage and will be your Marriage Pact.

*Remember*, it isn't important that you are in agreement on everything. What is important is that you discover now, in a relaxed atmosphere, where you don't agree and how you will cope with these differences.

For example: I assumed that I would not iron. Mike assumed that I would. We agreed that I would not do any ironing and that Mike would get rid of any clothes that needed ironing, send clothes out to be ironed or plan to iron them himself. Not exactly a compromise, but it worked for us!

Inherent in this agreement is Mike's agreement not to nag me about ironing because we agreed that I won't iron.

Had the agreement been that I would iron, it would have been my responsibility to do it without complaining. Mike would have had every right to expect the ironing to be done well and in a reasonable time frame.

Some of your discussion will be strictly informational and may not warrant an official agreement. You don't really need to agree that your partner's favorite color is blue, that his eyes are hazel or that her dress size is 10. You may, however, want to highlight these areas on your personal work sheets and keep them with your Marriage Pact for reference.

Only the two of you can decide which topics are informational. If either one of you feels strongly about a topic, it probably belongs in your agreements. I wanted a statement that I would not be expected to iron in our agreements, because I didn't want there to be any misunderstandings at a later date. You may not feel that strongly about a similar topic, but that's for you to work out.

When you come to a topic that is important to you for any reason, spend extra time on it and alert your partner to its significance.

A special topic for us was the *Emotions* category. Mike's son nicknamed him "Mellow Mike" because of his temper. Mike told me that if I could totally ignore his outbursts for ten minutes, it would all be over and he would no longer care about whatever set him off.

Although it has not always been easy, when I follow his advice, I am not drawn into his outbursts and they do not escalate into irrational arguments.

Be sure you want your partner to point out your failings
before you make it his job.

Carefully think through any *police authority* you give your spouse in your agreements. These are bound to be trouble spots later. It is easy when you are thin, healthy and full of good intentions to ask your spouse to nag you should you start slipping into bad habits like weight gain, lack of exercise or rising cholesterol levels.

It can be difficult to offer and accept support when the need arises. It will help if you agree now what you want your spouse to do when you have a problem. Using family members who have similar problems as bench marks can be helpful.

In our case, Mike's father had a stroke. His recovery was hindered by not following doctor's orders on exercise and diet. Should Mike have a stroke and take on his Dad's bad attitude, I am to do whatever it takes to coerce Mike into complying with doctor's orders; this includes any tactic that won't land me in jail!

When you encounter items on which you do not readily agree, you will need to negotiate a compromise. The *You Just Can't Win* chapter will give you additional direction in this area.

DON'T IGNORE ANY AREAS.

Care enough to communicate until you reach understanding. Negotiate until you reach an agreement.

It is very important that you either agree on an issue, agree on a compromised version, or agree how you will handle your disagreements. Whatever your final agreement, add it to your Marriage Pact and expect to live by it.

When your Marriage Pact is complete, sign and date it. Keep it in a safe place. Refer to it as needed for guidance.

Your Marriage Pact is a voluntary guide, not a legal document. If you have issues you want or need to make legally binding, have an attorney draft those documents *before* you get married.

## I Never Said That! And If I Did . . .

Don't fall to the temptation of reading the questions and discussing your answers while being "totally honest." Put your thoughts in writing. Compare your *written* comments.

We all want to please our loves and the temptation is ever present to say, "I agree" without concentrating on what's being said. Even if you know you are thinking things through and being honest, will you believe your partner when she agrees with you?

It can be especially important the more similar your ideas are. Your partner may believe that you are just being agreeable to please her.

The first time we grocery shopped together, I said, "Let's get vanilla sandwich creams, they're my favorite" and Mike said, "Mine, too." This happened in every aisle. We were so similar and got to laughing so hard I thought Mike was making fun of me. We'd probably been dating six months before I stopped buying vanilla sandwich creams for me and Oreos for Mike because, in spite of what he said, I *believed* he preferred chocolate.

Another problem is that we listen selectively and hear what we want to hear. "I hate football and can't stand having it on TV" may be heard by an avid football fan as, "I don't want to watch football with you." Football season arrives and you've got a problem. One of you is assuming that football will not be shown in your home, the other thinks it's OK to watch football all weekend as long as he plans to do it alone. Neither of you will be happy.

Do yourself a big favor, WRITE THINGS DOWN. BE SPECIFIC. Explore apparent differences thoroughly.

Sometimes you may agree on the essence of what someone says and yet disagree on the particulars. I knew that Mike wasn't big on fish. I thought we were in agreement since I'm not big on fish either: eating it once a month is about right for me. The first time I served fish I learned that what Mike really meant was, "You make me eat fish and you owe me."

Had we done a better job of exploring this issue, several unpleasant meals could have been avoided.

We cannot over-emphasize the importance of this part of the process. When we had about-to-be-married friends review drafts of this book, the majority did not commit their thoughts to writing. They claimed they'd had such a good talk about everything they didn't feel it was necessary. THEY'LL BE SORRY!

It may seem that the exciting days of your courtship will be etched in your mind forever. Unfortunately, time does a heck of a job of wreaking havoc on one's memory!

Do you remember what you talked about the last time you ate a meal together? Do you remember all the promises you've made to your partner? Do you remember the specifics of what you said the evening you decided you were really in love with her? Do you remember what was said and the circumstances of your last argument? If you think you do, sit down and try to recreate any of these conversations; I think you'll find that each of you remembers the situation differently. This will be especially true if there was a disagreement.

Think of your Marriage Pact as your personal Constitution and Bill of Rights. Can you imagine what a mess this country would be in if our founding fathers hadn't put our nation's documents in writing?

Eliminate misunderstandings. Put things in writing to verify your agreement or disagreement. In later months or years, when differences of opinion arise, it will be helpful to refer to your written notes to see if your feelings have changed.

In addition to helping you preserve your ideas through time, seeing things in writing lends credibility and the reassurance of your commitment to your thoughts. It will also help avoid comments such as, "I never said that! And if I did, that's not what I meant."

**Marriage is not a competition.
You win or lose together.**

# You Just Can't Win . . .

We believe that if two people want to get married, are willing to face their differences and are motivated to create a working marriage, they can successfully do it. The secret to their success will be their honesty in negotiating terms they are willing to live with and their integrity in abiding by their agreements.

While you want to reach agreement, be cautious not to force-fit your relationship with compromises you know you can't live with. It's important that you feel good about the decisions you reach, that you both maintain a caring attitude and that you feel each of you will be able to keep your side of the bargain.

Marriage is not a competition. There is no such thing as a winner and a loser. Either you both win or you both lose. For every argument that has a victor, a little piece of your marriage dies.

Work on an issue until you both feel like winners . . . or at least until neither one of you feels like a loser.

The most difficult part of any negotiation is identifying the real issue. Don't assume you know what your partner is thinking. Always ask "Why?"

Talk about the issue until you're sure you understand each other's position.

If, for example, you want to live in a condominium while your partner wants to live in a house, it may not be a problem.

Why do each of you feel that way?

.  It may be that you hate yard work but would live in a house if your spouse were willing to do all the yard work and outside maintenance.

.  Maybe your parents never did anything fun because they were always having to work around the house. In this case you might agree to put off a home purchase until you could afford to pay someone to do home maintenance tasks, or you might rent a home from an owner responsible for maintenance.

.  If your spouse's primary interest in a house is to have a garden, you might live in a condo and participate in a garden co-op.

There are no right or wrong solutions, but some solutions will work better for you. Your task is to propose alternate solutions until you hit on something you both think is reasonable and fair.

Sometimes you have strong opinions but don't know why. You want something, period. Set the topic aside and come back to it every thirty minutes or so, or every time you finish with another topic.

Think about the problem issue. Don't work at justifying why you are right to feel the way you do. Think back through your experiences with whatever is at issue and try to determine what makes you feel the way you do. There is a reason. Eventually it will become apparent to you. When it does, the depth of your emotion may surprise you. Share your feelings.

Once the real issues have been bared, you can begin searching for ways to fulfill the underlying needs in a mutually satisfactory way.

Sometimes it comes down to: *Who cares more?* If it's still a toss-up, set the issue aside and leave it until the end. You may find that you have several issues on which you're undecided. If this is the case, you may conclude that he gets to pick where you live and she gets to pick whether you live in a condo or a house. Although your friends may feel these categories are not equal, who cares? What matters is that the two of you feel satisfied that your agreements will work for both of you.

How you handle the momentary regrets that inevitably accompany a major decision will greatly impact your marital happiness. It's worked for us to be open about our regrets and for the other person to be supportive.

Occasionally I'll get maternal urges or Mike regrets our decision not to have children. Rather than brooding or feeling guilty, we talk about our feelings and do our best to comfort each other. By being open with each other, what began as a disagreement now draws us closer.

If you have significantly different views on issues that are very important to each of you, your task will be much harder. While we don't say it's impossible to successfully negotiate tremendous differences, you will both need absolute integrity and it will be critical that you trust each other implicitly.

If you cannot agree on areas that are deeply important to you, seek counsel from your clergy, a marriage counselor or other trusted professional before getting married. We believe that two people who love each other can work out most disagreements. However, agreement in some areas, such as having children or doing drugs are so fundamental to the success of a marriage that if you cannot reach an agreement you are possibly better off not getting married.

Problems which are ignored don't go away. They burrow in and fester and rear their heads sooner or later. Eventually you will have to deal with them. If you wait until the problems crop up in your marriage, they will be accompanied by a tremendous amount of tension and may result in divorce or bitter coexistence.

# I Think I Need Glasses . . .

After you're married, you sometimes see things
differently. A move to a new area, a significant change
in income, the birth of a child, a shift in work loads or
a well-intended but unrealistic agreement may have
repercussions that impact the viability of your Marriage
Pact. This is why it's a good idea to plan periodic
reviews of your agreements.

When you find that a portion of your Marriage Pact is
not working for you, change it. Use the same process you
used to develop your original pact, but limit your
discussions to those areas that aren't working as well as
expected.

If you have been communicating honestly and openly, problems will be obvious to both of you. Even so, reaching new agreements may not be easy.

Remember: You made a deal. It's not O.K. for you to decide an agreement isn't working and coerce your partner into accepting your terms. That's a sure way for one of you to lose - which means you both lose.

Since any change will impact both of you, you must concur that change is needed and agree on new terms. This is vital to keeping the spirit of your Marriage Pact and having it work for you.

**If you want to change an agreement, you
must gain your partner's approval without coercion.**

If you remember that you're a team and focus on working for your mutual benefit, it will be easier to resolve problems. You may find a trade off will make both of you happy, "If you let me off the hook on . . ., I'll agree not to hold you to . . . ."

We generally start by identifying the real issues and then work to resolve them creatively without bloodshed or bruised egos.

For example, we originally agreed that I was responsible for cooking and cleaning up the kitchen. Subsequently we agreed that I would go to night school. This makes it very inconvenient to cook and clean on those evenings. Even so, it's still my problem to handle the cooking and keep the kitchen clean because Mike is not willing to take on these responsibilities and we can't afford to pay someone to do them.

In working out a solution, we identified time as the issue from my perspective. From Mike's perspective the tasks themselves were the primary issues, but time was also an issue. We resolved it by compromising on the quality of the jobs: dishes sit in the sink for several days and school night dinners may be a bowl of cereal or a homemade TV dinner. Mike helps me with other tasks when time allows so I'm free to prepare meals in advance and have more free time to spend with him.

Again, there are no right or wrong solutions to problems.

You will face many choices in your marriage. Many couples use these to test their spouses, requiring them to prove their love repeatedly.

A well-constructed Marriage Pact can eliminate much of this push and pull. You have guidelines within which to make decisions and you know your rights and obligations.

If you've agreed that you will continue in your Thursday bowling league, your bowling on Thursday should neither be a source of hurt feelings nor a bone of contention. As long as the circumstances remain the same, there is really nothing to discuss.

When things change materially, you need to reevaluate your agreement. Say your team decides that to stay in the Thursday group you have to commit to practice on Tuesdays and Saturdays. It seems that your continued involvement should be renegotiated with your spouse.

You may find that you want to remove limits you've placed on your partner in your Marriage Pact.

One of our agreements was that I would stop attending self-improvement seminars. It irritated Mike that I didn't think I was as neat a person as he did. After several years of marriage, Mike saw a seminar brochure in the mail and decided that while it seemed like a waste of time and money to him, if I wanted to go, it should be my decision. We took that agreement off the list.

If you're not sure you want to permanently make a change, you might allow for a trial period. Be certain you write out the terms of the trial period to make sure there are no misunderstandings later.

Keep your Marriage Pact working for you. Taking it for granted or ignoring portions may erode the basis of your marriage.

When you got married you thought it was worth it.

Choose that it's still worth it.

# When Does Your Warranty Expire?

Did you ever buy anything that was guaranteed, but when a problem arose you found the guarantee wasn't worth the paper it was written on? Many people are expert in finding ways to get around their promises. As soon as their commitments aren't convenient, they suggest you read the fine print and excuse themselves from responsibility. Don't do this to each other.

Neither of you can eliminate this problem alone. Even if one of you is willing to give 200%, it won't make up for an uncommitted partner. It takes two committed individuals to safeguard a marriage.

Trust is central to the success of any relationship and fundamental in your marriage.

Do you trust your partner?

Do you believe he intends to live up to his commitments?

How about you? Can your partner trust you to keep your word?

There's a difference between upholding the letter of the law
and maintaining the spirit of your Marriage Pact.

When you marry, you pledge your love till death do you part. Hopefully that's a very long time. Your Marriage Pact should carry this same lifetime guarantee. Create only those agreements you believe are fair to both of you: agreements each of you feels you will be able to honor forever.

Many people will discuss issues, put their agreements in writing, and when they aren't convenient, they'll do what they please. Don't fall into this trap; it will undermine your relationship. And, if you give your partner authority to help you keep your agreements, don't hold it against them when they do!

Plan to live with your agreements even when it seems almost impossible. At times it will seem almost impossible.

Failure to keep promises leads to lies, guilt, shame and a need to distance yourself from the person you deceived. The damage you do may be irreparable - even if your spouse is willing and able to forgive you, you may be unable to forgive yourself.

The success of your marriage ultimately boils down to your integrity. Can your partner count on you to keep your word?

If your marriage is important to you, you can keep your word. Make it important.

## Say What You Mean, Mean What You Say

Your spouse wants to be part of the things in your life that make you happy. Here's another "Catch 22": How can your spouse make you happy when only you know what will please you at this point in time?

It is your job to let your spouse know how to make you happy in a given situation. Tell your spouse what you want. Be satisfied when he gives you what you asked for.

If you can keep communications this uncomplicated, it will greatly simplify your marriage.

Unfortunately, most people don't make communicating easy. They assume their spouse will be on the same wave length, will know how they feel and will know what they want them to do. This is just about impossible based on human nature!

At our best, we are not consistent. And while inconsistency is one of the things that makes us unique, fascinating and appealing, it can also make pleasing us very frustrating. For instance, sometimes when I'm upset I want to be left alone, occasionally I want to talk, other times I want to be held. How on earth is Mike supposed to know what I expect from him if I don't tell him?

When you want a specific response from your partner, preface your conversation with a statement that identifies how you're feeling and tells her what you want from her:

"I feel lousy. I need a hug."

"I feel lousy. I want to be left alone."

"I feel lousy. I want to talk while you comfort me."

If this sounds a bit simplistic to you, you are right! It's very simple and it works. Not only can it keep you from getting into trouble, it can help get you out of a sticky situation as the following example shows.

A friend was staying at our home when she learned of her sister's serious illness. She denied the news for two days and then fell apart. What she wanted was to be comforted by her husband. Unfortunately it was 2 am and her husband was across the country on a business trip. She did reach him, but the conversation was not soothing and reassuring. In fact it became a loud example of miscommunication. Her husband, jolted by the early morning call, expected someone to be dead. With his adrenaline flowing, he asked why she had to call in the middle of the night when she had already waited two days to tell him. She was defensive and tried to justify her actions.

I slipped a note in front of her, "Tell him you're very upset and you need his support." She pushed it away and proceeded to try to explain her situation. The conversation was escalating into an argument. Finally she said, "Well I just called because I needed your support." Things immediately simmered down. When off the phone she said, "Thank you. Even Bob couldn't resist an appeal for his support. But I hate playing games like that."

Our contention is that telling someone what you want is not game playing. Quite the opposite. Game playing is making someone guess what you want and what it will take to make you happy.

I believe she would have gotten the comfort and support she craved from his opening words had she started out by saying, "Bob, I'm very upset and I need your support."

Don't set each other up for failure. Ensure success. It's your job to get specific. Don't expect that anyone can guess your needs. They're *your* needs and they will change frequently. Keep your partner updated.

"I had a terrible day at work, would you please leave me alone for fifteen minutes so I can fall apart."

"I had the best day! Be happy for me!"

"I'm feeling sorry for myself and I just want you to listen while I complain."

"I'm really mad at Nancy. I want you to agree with me."

Sensitive issues? Preparing your spouse will preempt misunderstandings.

> "I need to talk but my feelings are so mixed up I'm sure everything's going to come out jumbled up. So I just want you to listen and not get upset cause I know this isn't going to come out right."

Need a reward? Don't hesitate to tell your partner!

> "I'm proud of myself. I fixed that faucet you've been reminding me about since last May. I could use a hug and a glass of lemonade."

Being specific will not only get you what you want, but will also give your partner the confidence of knowing she's done exactly the right thing. You both win.

Communicate completely. Give up any hidden agendas. When you ask for something, your spouse has the right to expect you to be happy when you get it.

If you're too beat to cook and ask your partner to pick up something for dinner on his way home from work, be satisfied with anything he selects. It's not his job to remember that six nights ago when you were at a sushi bar you mentioned, "Boy, this is my idea of a great carry out meal." If you want sushi, say so.

And if you say "Pick up a pizza," don't go feeling cheated if you get a medium when you wanted an extra large. Or if the pizza came from Little Italy and you wanted the house special from Tony's.

There's nothing wrong with wanting things done your way, but it's not fair to expect someone else to know what your way is today. If the details matter, say so!

**Avoiding a topic may create a problem where none existed.**

Some people say that what's not said is as important as what is said. If you want to have a terrific relationship, don't make that true for you. Don't make your spouse guess what's going on in your mind.

If you want to get an idea of how tough it is to know someone else's thoughts, try the following exercise. Have a conversation with your partner on any subject. When there is a pause, mentally guess what she is thinking, then ask her to tell you her thoughts.

The likelihood that your guess will be anywhere in the ballpark is remote. Complicate the issue with tension, fatigue, hunger or other strong emotions and it's easy to see why people miscommunicate.

It is equally important that you accept what is said at face value. Don't read between the lines.

If your spouse says he had a bad day at work and wants to be left alone, believe it. Don't assume he's still brooding over harsh words you had yesterday.

It's your partner's job to tell you what he's thinking and what he wants from you. It's your job to believe it and do your best to deliver what is wanted.

Keep it simple!

People don't get married because they want to irritate each other. They get married because they need each other and want to make each other happy. When you love someone, you are willing to do almost anything for her as long as you know it's what she wants you to do. This is true for you. It's true for your partner.

If you find yourself being irritated, identify what's going wrong and talk to your spouse. Believe that your partner doesn't want to be a thorn in your side . . . she just doesn't know how to be anything else.

If you remember that your spouse wants to be part of the things in your life that make you happy, it will make it easier to communicate effectively.

# Go Ahead. Make My Day!

During our wedding ceremony, the minister reminded us how easy it is to be excited about being married as you make plans and get married surrounded by family and friends. Retaining that enthusiasm, he warned, would take a conscious commitment to stay married to each other every day for the rest of our lives.

En route to the reception, we reminisced about the ceremony. The minister's talk had made sense to both of us. We had no idea how we would do it, but we agreed to recommit ourselves to our marriage daily. That night we stumbled across an unexpected solution.

Following the reception, Mike hung over the bathroom sink throwing up the effects of too many beers with tequila chasers. I was fuming. Cleaning vomit out of a sink was far from my image of marital bliss. But when Mike asked, "Do you still pick me?" it simplified things and put them in perspective. We laughed like idiots and began a new tradition.

Since that first day, we have picked each other every morning. We also reaffirm our love by picking each other every time we have a disagreement. And when one of us has been nasty, is feeling intimidated or emotionally undermined, or has disappointed the other, we ask, "Do you still pick me?"

This confirmation of our commitment to each other helps us keep the insignificance of our disagreements in perspective. Sometimes it takes one of us more than a few minutes to cool down enough to honestly answer, "Yes, I still pick you." But when you have been genuinely choosing that other person every day, you will want to say, "Yes, I still pick you."

"I pick you" are the three most important words in our marriage.

Say "I pick you" (or your own version) to each other every day. It may feel silly at first, but say it anyway. Give those words power. Choose to have them mean *I want to be here and I want you to be with me* and *I will abide by the agreements of our Marriage Pact.*

Choose each other every day. Say "I pick you" and mean it.

**Confirming your commitment helps keep things in perspective.**

This daily affirmation of choosing to stay married pays off:

- It's not as easy to take each other for granted.
- Knowing your spouse still chooses you over all others makes you feel good about yourself.
- It's easier to communicate with someone you know loves you in spite of your shortcomings.
- It's tough to deceive or cheat on someone when you pledge your love, trust and loyalty to them daily (We think this is so neat!)
- No need to wonder if everything is all right.
- It's easier to keep your side of the bargain because you rethink your commitment daily.
- When you argue, you still know you're loved.
- Removing self doubts encourages intimacy.
- You don't have to go looking for love when you know you're surrounded by it.
- It helps you maintain your perspective when you disagree.
- It will make your day!

We have consciously picked each other to be our marriage partner every day for nearly ten years. Over the years, the process has become something of a game, while the underlying sentiments have intensified with greater meaning.

If one of us sees it's after midnight, he'll say, "I pick you" to the other who then says, "I pick you, too." Our rule is that you can only pick each other for one calendar day at a time, so the earlier in the day you pick each other, the longer you get each other that day. We always race to see who picks first, sometimes teasing that the one who picked first must have wanted the other more.

When one of us travels, we pick each other daily in absentia and remind each other that "I pick you" when we make telephone contact.

Of course we still say "I love you," but we've found that saying "I pick you" means "I love you" and so much more.

# We're #1!

To ensure a great marriage, you need to decide that your relationship comes first.

We are all plagued with obligations to spend time (and money) with parents, friends, relatives, jobs, children, pets and hobbies. Make your spouse the most important earthly influence in your life and you'll be on your way to a richly satisfying life together.

If you choose to give your marriage top priority, it will be natural to choose to spend free time with your spouse.

If you devote three hours a week to watching sports on TV, doing needlework, working on a collection or tinkering in the garage, plan to spend at least three pleasurable hours a week sharing common non-sexual interests with your partner.

The fact that both of you are in the house or even in the same room doesn't mean you are spending time together. If one of you is reading the paper and the other is balancing the checkbook, you haven't spent time together even if you've been sitting side by side for four hours.

Time you spend doing chores or working on projects that demand your complete attention does not count as time together.

What do you like to do together? Take walks? Work in the garden? Go on picnics? Play cards? The key here is your mutual interests. If gardening is something you both enjoy, it counts; if it's a chore, it doesn't qualify.

You'll need to be honest with your partner about the satisfaction you derive from the different kinds of time you spend together. For some couples, enjoying a book in front of the fire or going out for dinner may be good quality time together. We don't consider those activities time spent together because we are both so intense that when we read or eat it takes all our attention and we hardly know the other exists.

When a demand for your time arises, you need to convince your spouse that this is a good use of your time. You must either agree that you will participate together or that you will take part alone. If you can't agree on your involvement, turn down the opportunity if you want to be happily married.

We are not advocating neglecting your family or friends by any means. We are saying that your spouse's feeling should come before theirs even if you feel your spouse is being a little unreasonable.

On a scale of 1-10, make your relationship a 10!

Everything comes down to choices. (Surprise!)

When people ask you to bake for a fund-raiser, fix their car, visit Aunt Mildred in the hospital or go out for dinner, they are asking you to give them more priority than you give your spouse.

No one extends an invitation so you can spend quality time with your spouse; they invite you to spend quality time with them. You must decide what's best for you - the two of you.

There will be times when you want to be surrounded by other people and there will be times when you need to be alone. It's unfortunate when your best friend's party comes on the first night the two of you have been home without commitments in two weeks. If it happens, we'd suggest that you call your friend and explain that you'll only be at the party for a short time. Make a brief appearance and then go home or out together. You need time alone together outside the bedroom.

To protect your relationships with your friends and family, try our simple insurance policy:

> If it's necessary to decline an invitation, always put the blame on yourself. Your family and friends will forgive you more readily than your spouse.

At the time it may seem easier to place the blame on your spouse: "I'd love to, but you know how my spouse feels about these things." This causes them to harbor hard feelings toward your spouse. Eventually, relationships with your friends or family may become so strained that you find yourself avoiding them.

You can always honestly say, "I'm sorry we won't be able to join you. We have a prior commitment." This is always true because you made a permanent commitment to each other when you married.

Your love for your children can make it very difficult to keep your spouse number one in your life. No matter how much you feel your child needs you, your spouse needs you more.

Some people will disagree with that statement. It's easy to look at a helpless infant and see their needs. Obviously, a very young child has physical needs that demand immediate attention. However, if you want to ensure that your children have a two parent family to grow up in, make certain that you give your spouse emotional priority.

Keep in mind that your primary job as a parent is to prepare your children for the world: to prepare them to live on their own without you! After they leave, you and your spouse will still need each other.

Putting your spouse ahead of your parents can be difficult. You have a lifetime invested with Mom and Dad and they are used to having priority in your life. You are not responsible for their happiness and they are not responsible for yours. If they love you, they will want you to be happy in your marriage. This means giving your marriage and your spouse top priority.

Hobbies, pets and jobs can also challenge a spouse's top billing. Don't allow them to precede your spouse.

Ultimately your spouse is all you have: your parents have their own lives, your children will grow into lives of their own; your friends will move away. You may lose your job, your pet will die, you may become blind or arthritic and no longer able to pursue your hobby. The one person whose life is really affected by you is your spouse.

Although it may be a tough adjustment for you, your family, your friends and your boss, you must make your spouse number one in your life if you want to be happily married.

# Thanks A Lot . . .

Being appreciative helps keep any relationship on an even keel. It involves taking a few minutes each day to remind yourself of the many small sacrifices your partner makes for you every day and letting her know you appreciate what she does for you.

Don't hesitate to give your spouse the gratitude you would accord a total stranger. If someone mowed your grass and wouldn't accept payment for his service, you would thank him profusely. Yet we often take for granted these same tasks performed by our spouse.

The fact that your spouse is supposed to do something doesn't take away from the fact that she does it. In fact, the task is probably much less agreeable because it is an obligation. Look at your life: any routine can be a boring unrewarding source of irritation.

Have you ever found yourself smiling as you help a friend do a chore that you hate to do at home? The task didn't change, your attitude did! Chances are your neighbor didn't expect you to do it and appreciated your efforts.

Making a special effort not to take each other's responsibilities for granted makes them more fun to do (or at least more bearable!).

Your spouse wants to make you happy. You want your spouse to be happy. It begins that simply. Things get messed up when you start keeping score.

If you want to be happy, never expect anything in return for anything you've done for your partner.

If you choose to look at each good turn done for you as a small gift to you, it will propel your marriage forward. If you choose to view things done for you as repayment of a debt, you will almost assuredly be miserable.

If being appreciative is not natural for you, don't despair. Taking someone's actions for granted is as much a habit as being appreciative. You can learn to be appreciative if you're motivated.

Every day, single out one thing that your spouse does that you're glad you don't have to do. It doesn't have to be a big deal, anything will do: getting up early, doing dishes, mowing the lawn, writing checks, walking the dog in bad weather, doing laundry, fixing the car, grocery shopping. Thank your spouse for making this contribution to your life. Although variety is nice, don't worry about finding something different every day; some things bear repeating.

Thanking your partner just for being who he is will put a smile on his face and a song in his heart. Take time to mention those things that attracted you to your spouse: that delightful sense of humor, any compelling physical attributes, mechanical prowess, beautiful manners, artistic abilities, craftsmanship . . . We all love to be reminded of how special we are.

Being appreciative always works. It improves morale and makes home a happier place to be.

Being appreciative creates a win-win situation.

Of course we all slip occasionally. Sometimes we aren't nice to each other, much less appreciative.

If you care deeply for each other and have made being appreciative a habit, spats won't last long and they won't leave scars. You may find it difficult to stay mad because you're so used to being supportive and appreciative that you'll want to do and say kind things to each other.

If you make appreciation a habit, it will work for you.

# If You Really Loved Me, You'd Eat Chinese

Take responsibility for making your marriage everything you'd hoped it would be. You can't force your partner to act on her love for you, but you can motivate yourself to act on your love for your mate.

A great trick is to use your love for your spouse to monitor your actions toward him. Regularly ask yourself, "Do my actions say *I love you*?"

The following example had wide-ranging impact on our marriage. We'd been married about three years when Mike and my Mom were discussing getting dinner from a carry-out place. Mike knew that Mom and I love Chinese food so he suggested that she pick up Chinese food for the two of us while he would make himself something. Mom didn't want anyone to have to cook so she offered to get Mike his favorite chicken.

At this point, Mike said, "This is crazy. If I had to cut off my arm to save Charlie's life, I wouldn't hesitate for a minute. Here I won't even eat Chinese food when I know that would give her so much pleasure. Forget the chicken. It's about time I learned to eat Chinese food."

Much to my surprise and delight, he did!

The domino effect an action like that has is amazing. Mike has worked to broaden his palate considerably - he even eats vegetables! This makes it more fun for me to cook; it also serves as a daily reminder of his love for me. And when I see him eating something he didn't eat before, it makes me want to do something special for him.

It's important to note that the initiative for the change had to come from Mike. Had I attempted to twist his love for me into a source of guilt or form of threat by saying, "If you really loved me, you'd eat Chinese," it would have led to harsh words. Believe me, Mike would not be eating Chinese food, broccoli or asparagus today.

Much of your happiness boils down to your perception of things. You choose your perceptions, so it's in your power to be happy in your marriage. Sounds overly simplistic? It works.

Mike has very sensitive toes and my size ten shoes manage to tread on his size twelves with uncanny regularity. In considerable pain, he used to give me a thorough tongue-lashing. One time when I stepped on his foot, he stood glaring at me, searching for the right zinger to tell me how clumsy I am. I blurted out, "I think that meant that I need a hug." Mike snickered and said, "Oh, excuse me, I must have misunderstood." After a bit of banter, he finally gave me a hug and a new meaning was given to the act of my treading on his toes. Now when I step on Mike's toes, he winces and then I say, "I guess I need a hug." We hug.

The circumstances didn't change, our perception did.

It's often the little things that sabotage happiness. You have the ability to turn those unpleasantries to your advantage. So do it.

Talents differ. Be appreciative.

Ultimately our concept is simple: You want a great marriage? Make your marriage great! Know that you make choices when you marry. Create a Marriage Pact that seems fair and livable to both of you. Work at staying married:

- have the integrity to live up to the agreements of your Marriage Pact even when it isn't convenient
- say what you mean and mean what you say
- choose to be married to each other every day
- make your spouse #1 in your life
- thank your spouse for being part of your life
- be happy with the choices you've made
- be happy with your spouse's best efforts, even when your spouse is not as capable as you wish or as good at something as you are yourself

It doesn't have to be complicated. Keep it simple. Love each other. Be happy.

# A Final Word . . .

Mr. B. I just want you to know that even though sometimes you've been a real pain in the butt on this project, I still pick you.

*Good.*

Do you still pick me?

*Yes.*

Even though I've awakened you dozens of times to tell you some hair-brained idea for this book?

*Yes.*

Even though you've eaten lots of cereal for dinner because I've been too busy to cook?

*Yes.*

Even though I've been cranky and irritable and ungroomed and single-minded and sat in front of my computer for hour after hour after hour?

*Yes.*

So say it.

*What?*

I want you to say you pick me.

*You pick me.*

You know what I mean, I want you to say, "I pick you."

*I pick you.*

Now say it like you mean it this time.

*I pick you.*

Really?

*Yes. I really pick you. I really, really, really, really pick you. I pick you today, tomorrow and forever.*

Hey, you can't do that. You can only pick one day at a time.

*Well, let's change the rules.*

No way! I want you picking me every day. It makes my heart happy. In fact I want to hear you say it again right now . . .

## <u>Write Us</u>

If you have ideas you'll share, we'd love to hear from you!

Were there any topics or specific questions you wish had been included?

Was there something you did to make the process of developing your Marriage Pact easier?

What special things do you do to keep your love fresh and your relationship special?

We'll share as many ideas as possible in future editions. We look forward to hearing from you!

**WRITE TO:**
**FAMILY MATTERS PUBLICATIONS**
**P.O.BOX 650, Dept. A**
**NORTH HOLLYWOOD, CA   91603**

To order additional copies of this book,
send $14.95 plus $2 shipping per book to:

Family Matters Publications
P.O. Box 650,  Dept. A
North Hollywood, CA   91603

MasterCard and Visa orders call (800) 762-8848

California residents add $1.01 tax.

Bulk rates are available.